TELL ME WHY, TELL ME HOW

HOW DO TADPOLES BECOME FROGS?

DARICE BAILER

 **Marshall Cavendish**
Benchmark
New York

Other Marshall Cavendish Offices:
Marshall Cavendish International (Asia) Private Limited, 1 New Industrial Road, Singapore 536196 • Marshall Cavendish International (Thailand) Co Ltd. 253 Asoke, 12th Flr, Sukhumvit 21 Road, Klongtoey Nua, Wattana, Bangkok 10110, Thailand • Marshall Cavendish (Malaysia) Sdn Bhd, Times Subang, Lot 46, Subang Hi-Tech Industrial Park, Batu Tiga, 40000 Shah Alam, Selangor Darul Ehsan, Malaysia

Marshall Cavendish is a trademark of Times Publishing Limited

All websites were available and accurate when this book was sent to press.

Library of Congress Cataloging-in-Publication Data
Bailer, Darice.
  How do tadpoles become frogs? / by Darice Bailer.
     p. cm. — (Tell me why, tell me how)
  Includes index.
  Summary: "Provides comprehensive information on the process of tadpoles changing into frogs"—Provided by publisher.
  ISBN 978-0-7614-4824-2
  1. Frogs—Life cycles—Juvenile literature. 2. Frogs—Metamorphosis—Juvenile literature. 3. Tadpoles—Juvenile literature. I. Title.
QL668.E2B276 2010
597.8'9156—dc22
2009023145

Photo research by Candlepants Incorporated

Cover Photo: Gail Shumway / Getty Images

The photographs in this book are used by permission and through the courtesy of:
Getty Images: Geoff Brightling, 1; Dorling Kindersley, 5; Gail Shumway, 6, ; Frank Greenaway, 7; George Grall, 8, 11; Martin Harvey, 10; Kim Taylor and Jane Burton, 13; Dr. Gilbert Twiest, 14; Robin Smith, 19; Gary Meszaros, 20. Alamy Images: cbimages, 4; Barrie Watts, 15. Minden Pictures: Derek Middleton, 12; Wil Meinderts, 16; Michael & Patricia Fogden, 17, 23; Gerry Ellis, 22; Mark Moffett, 24. Photo Researchers Inc.: Gusto, 18. Corbis: Michael & Patricia Fogden, 21, 25.

Editor: Joy Bean
Publisher: Michelle Bisson
Art Director: Anahid Hamparian
Series Designer: Alex Ferrari

Printed in Malaysia (T)
135642

CONTENTS

Like caterpillars that eat and grow and become butterfiles, these hungry tadpoles will become frogs one day.

Those Fabulous Frogs

Brown, speckled **tadpoles** dart through a cool pond. With chubby round heads and long tails, they look like tiny fish.

But these creatures are not fish. They are baby frogs! Like caterpillars that become butterflies, these tadpoles will go through a process called **metamorphosis**. When they become frogs, they will leap out of this pond and begin a new life on land—just like their ancestors did long ago.

This tadpole has grown back legs. It will soon lose its tail.

Frogs have been on Earth for about 200 million years. They were here before dinosaurs arrived, and they have not changed much since. Frogs evolved from fish into four-legged **vertebrates** that crawled onto land, perhaps to find food and to escape their enemies.

Frogs belong to a family of animals called amphibians. The word *amphibian* means "leading a double life." And it is true—most amphibians begin life in water and then live part-time on land.

There are about 5,360 kinds of frogs. Some come in very bright colors. Others have funny names, like the waxy monkey frog. The biggest frog in the world is the goliath frog of Africa. The goliath is about 1 foot (0.3 meter) long, and it weighs about 7 pounds (3.2

A red-eyed tree frog rests on a lily petal. The pads on its toes are very sticky and help the frog climb trees.

kilograms)—as heavy as a human baby! The gold frog of Brazil is one of the smallest frogs. It is smaller than a button.

Frogs live in rain forests and deserts and on mountains and plains. They survive on every continent except Antarctica. Frogs cannot live in this extremely cold place because they are cold-blooded, and they need the sun to warm them.

With two big eyes on top of their heads, frogs can see all around them. This helps them spot food and seek protection.

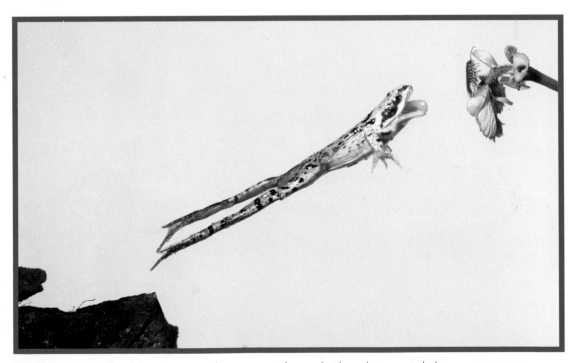

Frogs are excellent jumpers and can soar through the air to catch bugs or escape from enemies.

Frogs also have an excellent sense of hearing. Even more amazing, a frog uses its powerful legs to leap distances up to twenty times its length to snatch a cricket or to escape a crocodile.

Frogs that live in the **tropics** are small and colorful. Their skin is often poisonous, so their enemies learn to leave them

These blue poison dart frogs may look cute, but they are dangerous to touch.

alone. Other frogs can be as green as moss or as brown as leaves. These frogs can **camouflage** themselves to hide from **predators**.

Did you know that toads are in the frog family? Toads are usually shorter and fatter than frogs, and their skin is dry and bumpy. With their shorter back legs, toads cannot jump as high or far.

Some frogs burrow into sand to keep from overheating on hot days. They can spend months underground.

First Come the Eggs

During the cold winter months, frogs burrow in the mud or beneath logs. When spring arrives, they awaken and start to find mates.

At night, males puff up their throats to sing for the females. Each kind of frog sings its own special song. This helps it to find the right mate among hundreds of frogs. Male bullfrogs sing for female bullfrogs, and male peepers call out for female peepers.

From up to a mile away, females hear the males chirp, peep, croak, whistle, grunt, growl, bark, or scream. A carpenter frog sounds like it is hammering. A wood frog quacks. The Pacific tree frog says "ribbit." All together, it is a froggy chorus!

This male frog is puffing out its throat sac to sing for a mate. The sac is like a megaphone.

Some frogs jump up and down or dance to attract females. If a male frog sees a female frog swimming closer, it will crawl onto her back and hug her. The female is carrying eggs. The male holds onto the female and **fertilizes** her eggs as she lays them one by one. A female frog's skin can be slippery. One type of frog in South Africa produces a sticky glue on his stomach. The glue helps him stick to the female's back while they are mating.

Fertilizing the eggs may take a few hours, or even days. It depends on how many eggs the female frog lays. The tiny

A male frog hugs a female frog as he fertilizes her eggs.

Cuban frog lays a single egg, but the big American bullfrog releases 25,000 to 30,000 eggs at a time!

The eggs are tiny black dots covered with clear jelly. They are called frog **spawn**. There are no shells to keep the eggs from drying out, so frog eggs must be laid in ponds, lakes, or puddles on leaves. This keeps them wet and out of the reach of predators.

Frogs do not stay together after they mate, and most kinds of frogs leave the eggs to develop and hatch on their own. The eggs usually cluster together for warmth and protection. If they get too cold—or too hot—they will die.

Now I Know!
Why do male frogs sing?
To find a mate.

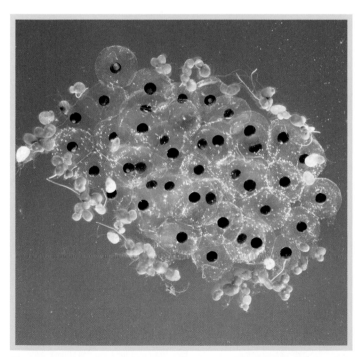

Frogs usually lay their eggs in water. The eggs glob together in cold water.

These tadples are ready to hatch from their eggs.

Here Come the Tadpoles!

Once the frog spawn are fertilized, they split into two cells. They continue splitting into more and more tiny cells until the little black dot starts to take form. Soon there is an oval-shaped body with a head and a tail, and the **embryo** begins to look like a tadpole.

Inside the egg, the tadpole's tiny heart is beating, and

The dark spot in this egg is a tadpole. The jelly around it is soft and clear.

there is egg **yolk** for it to eat. The jelly surrounding the tadpole keeps the egg from drying out and helps it float. The jelly lets water and oxygen flow in while it protects the tadpole from bumping into things.

Usually, the jelly tastes so bad that other creatures do not eat it, and the embryos are left to grow.

Most spawn hatch in one to three weeks. Some hatch in less than a week, while others might take over a year. When the eggs finally hatch, hundreds of tadpoles twist and wiggle free at the same time.

The baby frogs are called tadpoles or **pollywogs**. They look nothing like their parents. Less than a quarter of an inch long, the tadpoles are the size of a pencil eraser. Like fish, they breathe underwater through **gills**.

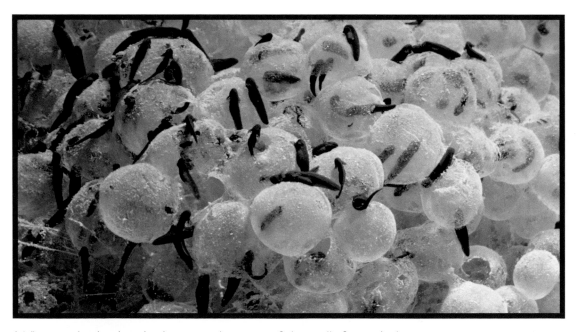

When tadpoles hatch, they eat the rest of the yolk from their eggs.

These tadpoles will become red-eyed tree frogs one day.

It will be three days before the tadpoles' tails develop and they can swim. During that time they rest at the bottom of the pond. The tadpoles hang on to plants and hide because danger lurks all around. There are hungry turtles, snakes, and fish ready to eat them. Sometimes even a tadpole's dad or siblings will eat it! Many tadpoles get eaten before they ever become frogs.

17

Tadpoles have suckers to attach
themselves to plants and tiny teeth
to scrape off food.

From Froglets to Frogs

Like hungry caterpillars, tadpoles eat a lot and grow quickly. They have tiny teeth to help them eat small plants. Tadpoles eat **algae** and pond **scum**.

At first, tadpoles breathe through gills that look like tiny feathers. A few days after hatching, flaps of skin grow over the gills. Then the tadpoles breathe **oxygen** through new gills inside their bodies.

These tadpoles must grow front legs before they can climb onto land.

As a tadpole changes into a frog, it grows back legs first. Two tiny bumps appear near the tadpole's tail. The bumps grow into legs. About eight weeks after hatching, a grass frog tadpole has hind legs with five webbed toes. Frogs thrust these legs back as they swim.

Next, the tadpole's gills are replaced by **lungs**. This will allow the future frog to breathe air through its nose on land. The tadpole now swims to the top of the water and gulps in air for the first time.

Soon, two new bumps appear. About twelve weeks after hatching, the grass frog tadpole has two front legs, each with four toes.

The tadpole's mouth widens, and it grows jaws and a long, sticky tongue. On land, frogs flick out their tongues to snatch a mouse or a grasshopper.

How long does it take a tadpole to become a frog? That depends on what kind of tadpole it is, how much food

In time, tadpoles begin to look more like frogs.

it has to survive, and how warm or cold it is outside. Cold temperatures slow down growth, and warmer temperatures speed it up.

A wood frog can change from a tadpole to a frog in a month. These frogs must grow quickly and leave home before their pond or puddle of water dries out. On the other hand, an American bullfrog tadpole takes about two years to become a frog. It is still in tadpole form when it **hibernates** during its first winter.

About sixteen weeks after hatching, many frogs climb out of the water. They are now **froglets**, or young frogs. A froglet might still have a tail stub, but it will get smaller and disappear. When the tail is gone, the metamorphosis is complete. In about one to three years, the frog will be an adult that can find its own mate and make tadpoles of its own.

This young tree frog will soon lose its tail and become a good jumper.

This eyelash leaf frog is growing inside its egg on land and will hatch as a frog instead of a tadpole.

Caring For the Young

Not all frogs begin life as tadpoles. There are about forty kinds of frogs that reproduce in very strange ways, especially in the tropics.

The eyelash leaf frog buries its eggs in a nest underground. The eggs skip the tadpole stage and hatch as froglets!

Marsupial frogs carry their eggs on their backs. The male Andean marsupial frog tucks the eggs in a pouch on the mom's back and fertilizes them there. The tadpoles hatch inside the pouch, and the female drops them in the water, where they finish growing.

Poison dart frogs also give their tadpoles a piggyback ride to water. For example, they might place the tadpoles in a

Tadpoles are growing inside eggs on the back of this marsupial frog.

little puddle on a leaf. Unusually, poison dart frog females lay eggs to feed to their tadpoles. These eggs are not fertilized. Instead, the eggs become baby food! Dart frogs feed their tadpoles every few days.

There was one frog that even used her stomach as a nursery! The gastric brooding frog of Australia swallowed as many as twenty fertilized eggs and kept them in her stomach. She stopped eating for up to two months while her eggs grew. Then her frogs hopped onto her tongue and out of her mouth. Scientists found this frog in the 1970s, but it has disappeared and may now be extinct.

A Darwin frog dad runs the nursery. He swallows his tadpoles and hides them in his

A golden poison frog carries her tadpoles to water.

vocal pouch until the froglets have grown up and hopped out.

Many frogs in North America live for several years. The larger the frog, the longer it survives. For example, some bullfrogs have lived for fifteen years. White's tree frog of Australia can live for more than twenty-one years.

Each spring, many adult frogs go back to the same ponds where they were tad-poles. There they sing and look for mates. Then there are new eggs, new tadpoles, and a new cycle of life.

Now I Know!

Which frogs feed their tadpoles unfertilized eggs?

Poison dart frogs.

This little Darwin's frog has just hopped out of its father's mouth.

25

Activity

Starting in March in most places, you can collect frog spawn and watch tadpoles grow right at home! Make sure you wash your hands well after touching pond water or amphibians.

1) Get a plastic bucket.

2) Go outside to a pond with an adult.

3) Look for eggs floating on the water. Fill your bucket with a little pond water, and gently push a few of the eggs into your bucket. Make sure you have plenty of pond water for them.

4) You can dump the eggs and pond water into a clear plastic container at home so you can see the eggs better. Do not add fresh tap water—it will kill them! You can use bottled spring water or faucet water that has sat on the counter for a few days.

5) At room temperature, most eggs will hatch in five to seven days.

6) You can feed your tadpoles lettuce that has been boiled and softened for a minute, small pieces of yolk from a hard-boiled egg, or powdered fish food.

7) Feed your tadpoles daily. Give them only what they will eat in a few minutes. Otherwise the water will get very dirty, and the tadpoles will not be able to survive.

8) Change the water each day by scooping out about a third of it and replacing it with new pond water, spring water, or old tap water.

9) Watch your tadpoles as they grow over the next two to three months. Keep a journal and write down what you see each day. It is very exciting to watch your tadpoles grow legs!

10) When your frogs have grown both sets of legs, take them back outside and set them free at the edge of a pond, where they can start their new life on land.

 Glossary

algae—Small, plantlike life forms that generally grow in water without roots or stems.

amphibians—Animals with backbones that live partly in freshwater and partly on land.

camouflage—To hide from predators by blending in with the environment.

embryo—An organism that is developing inside a fertilized egg.

fertilizes—Provides a female's egg with a male's liquid seed so that a new organism can grow inside the egg.

froglets—Frogs that have completed the metamorphosis from tadpoles and look like small adults.

gills—The organs on the side of a tadpole's head that help it breathe underwater.

hibernate—To go into a deep, sleeplike state.

lungs—Baglike organs that animals use to breathe air.

metamorphosis—The process that a frog goes through as it develops from an egg to a tadpole to an adult frog.

oxygen—A colorless and invisible gas that many organisms need to breathe.

pollywogs—Tadpoles.

predators—Animals that hunt other animals for food.

scum—A layer of film that grows on the surface of water.

spawn—The eggs laid by a frog.

tadpoles—Young frogs or toads that live underwater and breathe through gills like fish.

tropics—Hot, wet areas near the equator.

vertebrates—Animals that have backbones.

yolk—A part of an egg that has nutrients to feed a growing embryo.

Find Out More

BOOKS

Bishop, Nic. *Frogs*. New York: Scholastic, 2008.

Ganeri, Anita. *Frogs and Tadpoles*. North Mankato, MN: Smart Apple Media, 2008.

Kalman, Bobbie. *Tadpoles to Frogs*. New York: Crabtree Publishing Company, 2009.

Markle, Sandra. *Slippery, Slimy Baby Frogs*. New York: Walker & Company, 2006.

Moffett, Mark W. *Face to Face with Frogs*. Washington, DC: National Geographic Society, 2008.

Slade, Suzanne. *From Tadpole to Frog: Following the Life Cycle*. Minneapolis, MN: Picture Window Books, 2009.

WEBSITES

The American Museum of Natural History: Frogs: A Chorus of Colors
http://www.amnh.org/exhibitions/frogs/

Amphibiaweb: Hear different frog calls, right at your computer.
http://amphibiaweb.org/lists/sound.shtml

Arkive: Photos and facts about endangered frogs
http://www.arkive.org/threatened-species/amphibians

All about Frogs: Fun and weird facts about frogs
http://www.allaboutfrogs.org/

The San Diego Zoo: Amphibians
http://www.sandiegozoo.org/animalbytes/a-amphibians.html

Index

Page numbers in **boldface** are illustrations.